THE S

Published by Gallery Books
A Division of W H Smith Publishers Inc.
112 Madison Avenue
New York, New York 10016

Produced by
Brompton Books Corp.
15 Sherwood Place
Greenwich, CT 06830

ISBN 0-8317-7939-X

Printed in Hong Kong

10 9 8 7 6 5 4 3 2 1

OUTH

TEXT	D'ARCY RICHARDSON
DESIGN	DON LONGABUCCO

GALLERY BOOKS
An imprint of W.H. Smith Publishers Inc.
112 Madison Avenue
New York, New York 10016

The author extends many thanks to Miss Virginia Watson, Jim Walsh, Dave Brown, Allen Ashby, John Maier, and the Richardsons for their helpful suggestions and insightful comments. Thanks also to the tourism departments of Virginia, North Carolina, Georgia, Kentucky, and Tennessee. This book is dedicated to all my Southern friends and relatives.

3/4/5/6 The magnificent gardens at Tryon Palace in New Bern, North Carolina are designed in the eighteenth-century style. Completed in 1770, Tryon Palace was the residence of the royal governor and the meeting place of the colonial assembly.

INTRODUCTION

No other region of the United States has been as studied and discussed, written about, fought over, celebrated, and maligned as the South. What is it that sets the South apart? The history? The climate? The people? The landscape? The answer is all of these things together, for the whole of the South is greater than the sum of its parts. Nowhere else in this country is there a common history that binds all people—white, black, rich, and poor—to the land, to form a world that is uniquely Southern. The conflicts that brought down the Old South turned the world upside down for slave as well as master, and the legacy of the struggle to gain a new equilibrium has given the United States some of its best, if most painful, lessons in freedom and democracy.

More than anywhere else in America, the South is a state of mind. From the rolling hills of Virginia to the bayous of Louisiana, the people of the South exude a warmth to match the climate, where hospitality and politeness are a way of life. Adults are still addressed as "Sir" and "Ma'am," and extended families live close enough to visit on Sundays. Born during the reign of King Cotton, and nurtured into the present, the Southern culture is unique in the United States as a real product of its past.

The history of the South is as long and varied as that of the United States as a whole. Regions along the Atlantic coast were settled early by the British, who recognized the value of the temperate climate and the fertile soils. Tobacco and cotton became the mainstay of the economy, produced to feed the hungry factories of Britain. And, hand in hand with agricultural development, the social fabric of the South began to grow.

Slaves from Africa made the expansive plantations of the South possible, and their owners became rich and powerful. The leisure that this wealth afforded left time for grand parties in the ballrooms of magnificent plantation houses, hunts in the forests and fields, and a variety of other social functions that cemented the Southern aristocracy into a strong political, social, and economic force.

Along the Gulf Coast, the Spanish and French tried their hand at carving out a piece of the New World. The French traveled down the Mississippi, and the Spanish traveled up from Mexico, to establish the first settlements in the region we now call the Deep South. The coastal zones of Louisiana, Mississippi, and Alabama still bear the marks of these early forays in the language, food, and Creole and Cajun cultures of the area. Inland, colonists moved across from the Atlantic region to settle the Black Belt, known for its dark, rich soils. Here also King Cotton dominated the landscape.

The status quo was soon toppled. The Civil War had its genesis in a complex set of conflicts between North and South. For Southerners, the war was not just about slavery, although that was the rallying point for Northern abolitionists. To the South, slavery represented a way of life, as well as the basis of the region's economy. Southerners had long been dissatisfied with a growing disparity in regional wealth. Northern factories used the South's raw materials to amass fortunes on finished goods, and capital was slowly being drained away from the Southern economy. Frustration at this economic stranglehold, and the fierce pride and independence characteristic of Southern legislators, prompted them to invoke the notion of states' rights in a bid to save the region from economic ruin.

When the War came, the South suffered a defeat that continues to color every facet of Southern living.

The Civil War forever changed the face of the South, and all of its history is measured in relation to the four years of strife that effectively ended an era. To this day, the name of William Tecumseh Sherman inspires anger in the hearts of Southerners, whose ancestors witnessed his March to the Sea. With a contingent of 100,000 men, Sherman cut a wide swath from Virginia to Georgia, laying waste to the land and burning Atlanta to the ground. The years that followed saw the struggle to rebuild a devastated economy under the Union occupation and carpetbag rule. The South did recover, however slowly, but reminders of the War are everywhere, from battlefields to Confederate flags to holidays honoring Robert E. Lee and Jefferson Davis.

The New South moves in the syncopated rhythms of past and present. After the paroxysms of the Civil War and the civil rights era, the South has slowly begun to build a new tradition, mixing the glories of the past with present reality. There is a sense in the South that, from every window, the past is watching. Southerners raised in the traditions of their forefathers struggle with notions of how their lives measure up to those of their ancestors—when privileged Southern men and women reveled in the riches to be had from large plantations overflowing with cotton.

But today the South has new triumphs to celebrate. The richness of its cultural heritage, the warmth of its citizens, and the social and economic revolution that has taken place since the Civil War have fostered a New South with traditions even prouder than those of King Cotton. The collective Southern conscience, still working through mistakes made in the past, has produced some of the finest writers this nation has read. Thomas Wolfe, Tennessee Williams, William Faulkner, Richard Wright, James Agee, and Eudora Welty are but a few of the many writers who put into words the struggles of the South and its citizens to come to grips with what it means to be Southern in a rapidly changing world. Of equal import are the leaders that Southern culture produced, including such champions of equal rights as Abraham Lincoln, Cassius Marcellus Clay, Booker T. Washington, and Martin Luther King, Jr. Today, their efforts are slowly bearing fruit as the black community gains an increasing voice in the political life of the South. Governor Douglas Wilder of Virginia, Mayor Andrew Young of Atlanta, and Harvey Gantt of North Carolina are forging the way for a new Southern revolution, in which the voices of all citizens are heard with equal respect.

While the South has shed many of its objectionable and outdated customs, it has managed to retain the charm and hospitality for which it became famous in earlier times. The warmth of the climate dispels the sense of urgency one might feel in other sections of the country, and Southern life flows by like the lazy waters of the Suwannee River. Southerners are a gregarious lot, possessed of a special gift of gab—no conversation can end before the entire litany of relatives and friends has been inquired after, and their health and happiness assured. This friendliness lends itself to long afternoons on the porch swing, coupled with copious amounts of iced tea or lemonade to stave off the steamy summer sun.

At mealtimes, Southerners maintain their peculiarities with culinary concoctions dating from plantation days. Cornbread, country ham and biscuits with red-eye gravy, grits, greens, fried chicken, barbecue, and warm deep-dish cobblers satisfy the Southern palate. Down on the bayous, the cuisine heats up as the Cajuns and Creoles add tabasco and secret spices to fresh-caught seafood. And over Kentucky way, the mysterious state dish is burgoo—a stew made with 'coon or 'possum and varied other ingredients, much like that which the pioneers tasted after a successful hunt. Like most other everyday occurrences, mealtimes are not just for eating but for socializing as well, and no better occasion can be found than a pig roast, barbecue, or crawfish boil to find out what's happening with the neighbors.

The landscape of the South is as welcoming as its inhabitants. Here, you won't find the imposing crags of the West or the flatness of the Plains. The Appalachians have been worn into gentle, rolling hills with verdant valleys in between. The Blue Ridge and the Smokies are mountain getaways for Southerners seeking solitude and a breath of fresh air. Other geographical features are known by such friendly names as the piney woods, the sandy hills, and the pennyrile. Water abounds, and recreational activities center around the lakes, streams, rivers, and ocean beaches.

The states of the South—Virginia, Tennessee, Kentucky, North Carolina, South Carolina, Georgia, Alabama, Mississippi, and Louisiana—are as winsome as the belles at a debutante ball, each with a particular charm of her own. As Ralph McGill has so astutely observed, there are many Souths, and the choice is that of the visitor. Travel through the South and seek out the haunts of pioneers and pirates, stroll down live oak avenues to antebellum plantation houses, and take in the beauty of magnolias and azaleas in bloom, or the bounty of peaches, pecans, and peanuts. Every Southern experience will be different, but no matter where you roam, the welcoming smiles and dulcet tones of Southern accents are discoveries to be savored in a world that often travels by too fast.

VIRGINIA: THE OLD DOMINION

The *grande dame* of the Southern states, the progenitor of presidents, Virginia is a special blend of history, charm, and natural beauty. The Old Dominion's aristocratic past is steeped in the lore of our founding fathers—Washington, Jefferson, Madison, and Monroe. It was in Jamestown in 1607 that British colonists first gained a tiny foothold in the New World. Thanks to John Rolfe's tobacco plants and his marriage to Pocahontas, Virginia grew into a prosperous agricultural settlement as colonists moved up the rivers and into the Piedmont to establish plantations on the fertile soils. In 1619, the Virginia planters sat down to the first real American Thanksgiving at Berkeley Plantation along the James River, two years before the famed Plymouth Pilgrims' Massachusetts feast. In time, ambitious planters populated the length of Virginia's coastal Tidewater, from Jamestown in the south to the Chesapeake Bay, while German and Scotch-Irish settlers from Pennsylvania moved into the Valley of Virginia to cultivate their small farms in the shadow of the Blue Ridge. Spurred by the influx of slaves in the 1700s, Virginia grew to be the largest and wealthiest of the colonies.

Virginia's prosperity lasted until the Civil War. Loath to secede from the Union she had fostered, Virginia's decision to throw her support to the Confederacy is at once a testimonial to the common heritage that binds the South and a condemnation of the great power wielded by the plantation aristocracy. Virginia paid a heavy price for her Southern allegiance—more than half of the battles of the Civil War were fought on Virginia soil. It was at Appomattox Court House on Palm Sunday, 1865, that Robert E. Lee, that fine Southern gentleman, surrendered his 1st Army of Virginia to a magnanimous Ulysses S. Grant.

Virginia has since grown into a modern, industrial state, but not without its quiet spaces. Far from the high-tech bustle of northern Virginia, the shipyards of Newport News, the tobacco factories of Richmond, and the cotton mills of Danville, the heart of the Old Dominion lives on—in the rolling pastureland, stately mansions, small towns, and ways of life of farming folk. This is the land of the real Virginia, with acres of thoroughbred farms, beef cattle, feed corn, and apples; where you wake up on a dewy summer morning to the scent of honeysuckle growing on the fence, and where the residents still claim our nation's most famous citizens as their forebears.

Virginia carries on its traditions, most notably the fox hunting and steeplechase racing for which the northern horse country is famous. In the south, tobacco fields still spread through the Piedmont, and the rural way of life remains central to the culture. Along the spine of the Blue Ridge, Virginia's prime natural attraction, the Blue Ridge Parkway carries thousands of Carolina-bound visitors eager to see the spring blooms or the breathtaking fall display. The Tidewater's treasures include Chincoteague and Assateague Islands National Wildlife Refuge, the famous crabbers of the Chesapeake Bay, and the summertime student mecca of Virginia Beach. And, of course, historic attractions abound—from the restored colonial hub of Williamsburg and the plantation homes along the James to the numerous Civil War battlefields and the Confederate capital at Richmond, Virginia inspires a sense of our nation's finest and most infamous moments.

15 Ever the individualist, Thomas Jefferson broke with the traditional Georgian architecture of the colonies and brought neoclassical design to the New World. Monticello, his pride and joy, is the embodiment of Jefferson's spirit.

16/17 Robert E. Lee surrendered his Confederate forces at Appomattox Court House, ending the bloody conflict of the Civil War. Today, Appomattox is a National Historic Site.

18 Chincoteague National Wildlife Refuge off the Delmarva Peninsula is home to wild ponies and many species of birds.

19 The 300 wild ponies of Assateague and Chincoteague Islands, made famous in Misty of Chincoteague, are rumored to be ship-wrecked descendants of Spanish galleon stock. Every year, the ponies are rounded up during Pony Penning Day on Chincoteague, and some are auctioned off to families to pre-vent overpopulation.

20 Shellfishing on the Chesapeake Bay is an important money-maker for Eastern Shore dwellers. These skipjacks are harvesting oysters.

21 top Virginia Beach draws throngs of visitors in the summer, including many students who work in the hotels and restaurants that line the shore.

21 bottom The Hampton Roads area, including Newport News, Norfolk, Portsmouth and Hampton, is a military and ship-building center. Visitors get a look at the Atlantic and Mediterranean fleets on a tour of the harbor at Newport News, which boasts one of the largest shipyards in the world.

22/23 The Tunnel Overlook in Shenandoah National Park provides a panoramic view of the Blue Ridge Mountains.

24/25 A light snow blankets Mabry Mill along the Blue Ridge Parkway. Noted for its natural beauty, the Parkway runs 469 miles from Shenandoah National Park at Front Royal to the Great Smoky Mountains National Park.

26 Virginians still carry on with some of their British traditions. Fox hunting in the fall and steeplechase racing during the spring keep Virginians busy in the stables of the hunt country.

27 top The Shenandoah Valley, known for its fertile soils and rolling pasturelands, produces five million bushels of sweet Virginia apples per year.

27 bottom The Princesses of Winchester's Apple Blossom Festival float by during the annual parade in May. Winchester is Virginia's self-proclaimed "Apple Capital."

28 The Governor's Palace in Colonial Williamsburg was home to Patrick Henry and Thomas Jefferson in their terms as the first and second governors of the Commonwealth, as well as to seven royal colonial governors before them. The boxwood maze behind the Palace is a major attraction for adventurous visitors.

29 An enthusiastic crowd of listeners and picnickers enjoys a performance at Wolf Trap Farm Park in Vienna. The park is dedicated to the performing arts.

30/31 The warm hues of autumn delight visitors to the George Washington National Forest.

32/33 Mindful of the need to provide education to Virginia's citizens, Thomas Jefferson and friends chartered the University of Virginia in 1819. It opened its doors in 1825, and has since become a leading institution of higher learning. Jefferson himself designed the original portion of the campus shown here.

34 The colonial houses and cobblestone streets of Old Town Alexandria remind residents of the famous footsteps that traced similar paths during the nation's birth.

35 Virginians stage one of the annual re-enactments of an important Civil War battle at Alexandria.

36 *The* Susan Constant, Godspeed, *and* Discovery *brought just over 100 British colonists to Jamestown in 1607, establishing the first permanent English settlement in the New World. These replicas are moored at the James River dock in the restored village, now a National Historical Park.*

37 *The plantation home of George Washington overlooks the Potomac River south of Washington, D.C. More visitors flock to Mount Vernon each year than to any other historic home in the country.*

KENTUCKY AND TENNESSEE: THE FRONTIER

When Daniel Boone and his compatriots stood at the Cumberland Gap in the late 1700s, they saw a land of rolling hills and expansive forests. This was the next frontier for the settlers of the New World, a land far removed from the comforts of colonial settlements along the coast and goods from the Motherland. Less fortunate settlers, who had not been granted vast tracts of land for plantations of their own, were eager to make their way to this new land of opportunity across the Appalachian range.

Geographically isolated from the rest of the colonies, Kentucky and Tennessee developed their own Southern style, tempered by the harsh realities of frontier living. The eastern areas were populated by mountain folk who hunted and trapped. In later years, after the Indians succumbed to the onslaught of pioneers and, finally, to Andrew Jackson's forces, the way was paved for a flood of new settlers in search of more fertile soils and unclaimed lands. Aristocrats from Virginia joined the exodus, making their way past the mountains and into the lowlands to establish new plantations of tobacco and cotton, and to breed the horses still famous today.

The difference in mountain and lowland lifestyles created serious divisions within the states during the Civil War. Mountain dwellers, who owned no slaves and had no stake in the slave-based economy, generally sided with the Union, while the plantation aristocracy fought with the rebels. Although Kentucky attempted to remain neutral, and did not in fact secede, Kentuckians were drawn into the fray on both sides. Tennessee was equally divided in its sentiments. Andrew Johnson, senator from Tennessee, was the only Southern legislator to remain in Congress during the War, earning himself the Vice Presidency under Lincoln for his loyalty.

Today, Kentucky and Tennessee conjure up images of horses, bourbon, music, and mountains. The same dichotomy that split the states during the Civil War can still be seen today in the distinct regional characters. The mountains are still the haunt of coal miners and the descendants of the original pioneers, the likes of the Hatfields and McCoys. The Appalachians have given us bluegrass music, moonshine, mountain crafts, and memories of more simple pleasures. Visitors flock to the Smokies to relax and to fish the mountain streams.

In the flatlands, thoroughbreds graze on the phosphorous-rich bluegrass, Tennessee Walking Horses stride gracefully through the pastures, and country music is cultivated in the clubs of Nashville while the fields are planted with cotton, tobacco, corn, and hay.

The western lands are dominated by the mighty waters of the Ohio, Tennessee, and Mississippi rivers. The Tennessee Valley Authority tamed the Tennessee and revived the ailing economy of the region during the Depression by creating a series of dams to form a vast and beautiful recreation area centered around the Land Between the Lakes region on the Kentucky-Tennessee border. At the edge of the Mississippi, Memphis lays claim to the blues and the beginnings of rock and roll. Stroll down the street to Sun Studios, where Sam Phillips started young Elvis Presley on the road to fame by recording "That's All Right Mama," or drop by W.C. Handy's house on Beale Street.

Wherever you go, the Southern frontier is full of the hospitality for which the South is famous. From the genteel ways of the horse country to the down-home neighborliness of the hills, Tennessee and Kentucky combine tradition and pioneer spirit into their own special brand of Southern living.

39 Horse breeding has been an integral part of Kentucky life since colonial days. These thoroughbreds are grazing on the bluegrass at Stonereath Farm in Bourbon County.

40/41 The sun sets over a typical scene outside of Knoxville.

42 The United Society of Believers in Christ's Second Appearing, better known as the Shakers, formed several communities in Kentucky in the 1800's, including this one in Pleasant Hill. The Shakers, famous for their furniture-making skills, adhered to the principles of simplicity, pacifism, celibacy, and isolation from the rest of society.

43 This elegant memorial in Hodgenville, Kentucky shelters the humble one-room log cabin where Abraham Lincoln was born on February 12, 1809. Lincoln's arch rival, Jefferson Davis, was born a little farther west, in Hopkinsville, in 1808.

44 The best known sight in Kentucky, Churchill
Downs' twin spires preside over the track
where the bluebloods of the thoroughbred
world run for the roses during the Kentucky
Derby in Louisville. The Derby has been run
over this course since 1875.

45 Stephen C. Foster's "My Old Kentucky
Home" was inspired by Federal Hill in
Bardstown, where he often visited his cousins.

46 Elvis Presley's final resting place is located on the grounds of his Memphis mansion, Graceland. Thousands of fans from every corner of the globe come to pay their respects each year.

47 A statue of the King of Rock 'n' Roll looks down on Beale Street. Born in Tupelo, Mississippi, Elvis became as famous for his pelvic gyrations as for his gold and platinum singles.

48/49 Tennessee and Kentucky share the Land Between the Lakes area, a 170,000-acre recreation area. Created by the Tennessee Valley Authority during the New Deal era, the Land Between the Lakes is a popular destination for Southern fishermen, boaters, hunters, and hikers. This photo shows Lake Cumberland at sunset.

50/51 Daniel Boone first led settlers from North Carolina and Virginia through the Cumberland Gap in the 1770s, opening the Kentucky-Tennessee frontier.

52 top Clarence Moorehead waits for the Tennessee sour mash to age at the Jack Daniels Distillery in Lynchburg. Whether it's in a mint julep or served with some branch water, whiskey from Tennessee and Kentucky is a distinctly Southern treat.

52 bottom A band serves up some foot-stompin' bluegrass at one of the numerous festivals that celebrate the native brand of music. Born in Kentucky and nurtured throughout the Appalachians, bluegrass is winning larger audiences with its infectious high spirits.

53 The mountain people of the Appalachians have breathed new life into their old ways. Once a matter of survival, the practicing of traditional mountain crafts, including quilting and weaving, draws tourist dollars to the historically poorer areas of the region.

54/55 Known for its low-hanging clouds and black bears, the Great Smoky Mountains National Park along the Tennessee-North Carolina border is the nation's most visited park. The small foothill communities of Gatlinburg and Pigeon Forge have boomed as resorts spring up to take advantage of an ever-increasing flow of tourists.

56 A family enjoys the beauty of Laurel Falls in the Great Smoky Mountains National Park.

57 top Glenn Miller first played "Chattanooga Choo-Choo" in the film Sun Valley Serenade in 1941. This modern-day miniature choo-choo, a tribute to Chattanooga's railroad history, runs around the former Southern Railroad Terminal, now a complex of hotels, shops, restaurants, and museums.

57 bottom True to its name, Kentucky's Mammoth Cave is the world's longest-known cave system, numbering 300 miles of explored passageways. The area between Louisville and Bowling Green, known as Cave Country, contains hundreds of caves.

58 W.C. Handy gave birth to the blues in the run-down bars of Beale Street in Memphis. Beale Street today supports a lively nightlife, with clubs and outdoor musical entertainment.

59 The Grand Ole Opry has broadcast live from Nashville, 52 weekends a year, since 1925. Most all of country music's greats have passed through the Opry at one point or another in their careers, and Nashville remains the center of the country music industry.

60/61 The annual Summer Lights festival enlivens the Legislative Plaza in Nashville.

NORTH CAROLINA, SOUTH CAROLINA, AND GEORGIA: THE ATLANTIC COAST

When the British first turned their attention to the New World, their gaze fell on the promising coastline of the Carolinas. Sir Walter Raleigh's ambitions were realized when a group of colonists, led by Governor John White, established a settlement on Roanoke Island in 1587. The Governor's granddaughter, Virginia Dare, was the first British child born in the New World. When supplies dwindled, Governor White left the fledgling colony and sailed back to England to restock, only to return several years later to a deserted settlement. The fate of the Lost Colony remains a mystery.

The British were not the first to try and fail at colonization of the area. The French and Spanish before them had sent colonists and missionaries to the coast of Carolina and Georgia, but with no success. It was not until King Charles II granted the Lords Proprietors the land south of Virginia, in exchange for their political favor, that permanent settlements appeared. Carolina, as it was then known, was settled in the south by British transplants who made their way to Charleston. The north was settled not by sea, but by the migration of other colonists who were joined in later years by French Huguenots, Swiss, Scotch-Irish, German, and Welsh settlers. Carolina's burgeoning population led to its division into North and South Carolina in 1712.

Meanwhile, James Oglethorpe was petitioning King George II for some land in the colonies to establish a new home for debtors locked in the wretched prisons of England. Georgia, the last of the original thirteen colonies, was founded in 1733 at Savannah.

The colonies flourished until the Civil War, fueled by the labor of thousands of slaves who worked vast tracts of cotton and tobacco. The glorious age of plantation living came to a close, however, when Confederate forces aimed the first shots of the Civil War at the Union garrison at Fort Sumter, South Carolina, on April 12, 1861. Four years of fighting ravaged the states, culminating in Sherman's infamous March to the Sea and the burning of Atlanta on September 2, 1864. The states' struggle under Union occupation and carpetbag rule continued during Reconstruction.

Since then, the Atlantic states have grown into the hub of the New South. Fads and finance revolve around trends set in Atlanta, a recognized center of culture and international business. Scientific advances are made at the world-renowned Research Triangle Park in North Carolina. Furniture, textiles, lumber, naval stores and produce are shipped to distant markets from the forests and croplands.

As in the rest of the South, however, the Atlantic states gain their characters not just from their cities and towns, but also from the spaces in between. They are endowed with a coastline of immense beauty and tranquility, from the Outer Banks of North Carolina to the Sea Islands of South Carolina and the Golden Isles of Georgia. The Outer Banks were the hiding place of Blackbeard, who made his home at Bath, and the site of the Wright brothers' historic Kitty Hawk flight. Along the Sea Islands, the curious Gullah dialect still in use is a remnant from plantation days, when slaves wove their African words into the English they spoke. Georgia's Golden Isles introduced golf to the New World, when Scottish Highlanders first drove balls near Darien. Inland, the fields and forests meet the mountains. Georgia marks the start of the Appalachian Trail that runs all the way to Maine, and North Carolina shares the Smokies with neighboring Tennessee.

North Carolina, South Carolina, and Georgia are the midlands of Dixie, and the embodiment of classic South. Here reside the plantation homes, magnolias, and debutantes of days gone by. The citizens of the New South may greet their future willingly, but always with an eye toward their common past.

63 A wedding carriage rolls through the quiet streets of old Charleston, much as it was in the days before fossil fuel.

64/65 Charleston's Rainbow Row boasts an array of pastel houses that date from the 1740s. Fourteen private homes line the waterfront along East Bay Street.

66 Woodrow Wilson married Ellen Axson, the pastor's granddaughter, at the Independent Presbyterian Church of Savannah in 1885. Churches are still an important meetingplace for members of all Southern communities.

67 Millionaires from the North bought Jekyll Island as a private winter hideaway in 1886, and vacationed there until the beginning of World War II. The clubhouse was built in 1887 to house club members, but individual "cottages" sprang up to afford more privacy for their occupants. Now the island is a popular vacation spot owned by the State of Georgia.

68/69 George C. Vanderbilt's opulent Biltmore Estate near Asheville, North Carolina was constructed in the 1890s. The estate comprises 12,000 acres in the Blue Ridge Mountains.

70/71 The quintessence of Southern plantations, Boone Hall near Charleston is famous for its 250-year-old Avenue of Oaks, stretching three-quarters of a mile to the plantation house. The plantation, which produced cotton and then pecans, now produces successful takes for movie moguls, and was featured in Gone with the Wind.

72 Covering almost 700 square miles, the Okefenokee Swamp in south Georgia is home to alligators, deer, bear, raccoons, birds, and cypress trees. The basin, named by the Seminole Indians as "land of the trembling earth," is constantly washed by the waters of the Suwannee and St. Mary's rivers.

73 A windsurfer goes airborne in front of the Cape Hatteras Lighthouse on the Outer Banks in North Carolina. Built of brick in 1870, the lighthouse is the tallest in America.

74/75 A hang gliding neophyte tries his luck off Jockey's Ridge in Nags Head, North Carolina, just a stone's throw from Kitty Hawk where Wilbur and Orville Wright made their first flight on December 17, 1903. Jockey's Ridge, a product of beach erosion and strong winds, is the highest sand dune in North America.

76/77 A popular southern pastime is enjoyed on the piers of the Outer Banks.

78 North Carolinians' obsession with college basketball is fueled by the successes of the Duke and UNC squads. Here Duke meets Virginia at Cameron Indoor Stadium on the Duke campus.

79 Harbour Town Golf Links, one of the top 100 courses in the world, was designed with the help of Jack Nicklaus. This Scottish-style course is one of three at the exclusive Sea Pines Resort on Hilton Head Island.

80 Although the South is growing rapidly, rural scenes such as this are still the rule rather than the exception.

81 Still the number one crop in North and South Carolina, tobacco faces stiff opposition in the political arena as legislators seek to counter the powerful tobacco lobby.

82/83 Country stores like this one near Helen, Georgia are part of the landscape of virtually every small Southern town. Country stores continue to provide food, drink, and conversation to a regular cast of local characters.

84/85 Only 27 years old when Sherman's army burned it to the ground, Atlanta rose like a phoenix (as the oft-quoted saying goes) to become the hub of the New South. Although still Southern in its roots, Atlanta now means business to corporations from around the world.

86 The juxtaposition of old and new in Atlanta embodies the South's struggle to reconcile its slow-paced past with an increasingly frenetic future.

87 The Westin Peachtree Plaza in Atlanta, America's tallest hotel, boasts the inner atrium design that was born in Atlanta at the nearby Hyatt Regency, designed by John Portman. Atlanta does a booming convention business, and hotels form an integral part of the downtown economy as well as its skyline.

ALABAMA AND MISSISSIPPI: THE DEEP SOUTH

The first Spanish explorers to set foot in the territory around the Mississippi River stayed only long enough to ascertain that this steamy landscape was void of gold. The area was largely neglected until westward-roving British settlers threatened to encroach upon France's holdings, prompting the bold Frenchman La Salle to sail down the Mississippi from Canada and claim the river's entire drainage for his king in 1682. Thus began the colonial confusion from which the states of Alabama and Mississippi were born. In the ensuing century, the region passed between France, Britain, and Spain before the United States negotiated a settlement for the whole of the Mississippi Territory in 1798.

But the way was not yet cleared for the flood of eager pioneers from the Atlantic states: Cherokees, Choctaws, Chickasaws, and Creeks prospered in the area, with towns and agricultural systems of their own. The clashes between displaced Indians and would-be landowners along Alabama's frontier escalated into the bloody Creek War, ending with Andrew Jackson's defeat of Indian forces at the Battle of Horseshoe Bend in 1814. The resultant treaties forced the Indians to relinquish all claims to the land, and they joined their brethren from Kentucky and Tennessee on the exodus to Oklahoma, along the Trail of Tears. Virginians, Tennesseans, Carolinians, and Georgians quickly erased all reminders of the flourishing Indian culture, replacing it with vast fields of cotton and opulent plantation houses. The Deep South began to take root in the dark, fertile soils of the Black Belt.

This was the land where King Cotton dictated social as well as economic development, where plantation owners depended on the labor of thousands of slaves for their wealth and position. Increasing abolitionist sentiment threatened to destroy the planters' paradise, and bitter resentments ran deep at the outset of the Civil War. The final nail was hammered into the Confederate coffin when Grant took Vicksburg on July 4, 1863, giving the Union control of Mississippi River supply routes.

Alabama, the self-proclaimed "Heart of Dixie," has grown into an important manufacturing and high-tech center, as well as a popular vacation spot for visitors seeking any number of diversions. In Montgomery, you can take a trip through history by visiting the capitol building where the Confederacy was born, or head over to Dexter Avenue, birthplace of the civil rights movement. With more miles of waterways than any other state in the Union, Alabama offers fishing, whitewater rafting, and swimming amidst serene landscapes of rolling hills and valleys. And in Mobile, you can take part in the country's oldest Mardi Gras festival, a tradition started by the first French colonists.

In Mississippi, the annual blessing of the shrimp fleet in Biloxi attests to the importance of the fishing industry in the state. The home of William Faulkner and the birthplace of Elvis Presley are popular destinations. In the north lies more ancient history, where a wealth of Indian artifacts and mastodon skeletons have been uncovered by archaeologists.

Picking up where the rest of the South leaves off, Alabama and Mississippi are quintessential South. Thick Southern drawls interrupt bites of barbecue, the humid air hangs over the cotton fields, and night crawlers wait on hooks for careless fish. The Deep South has many treasures to be discovered, but none so precious as the warmth of its citizens and their ability to make visitors feel right at home with their slow Southern rhythms.

89 Now relegated to recreational status, riverboats like the Mississippi Queen were once the critical link between upriver cotton plantations and markets in the coastal port cities. In their heyday, steamboats were the floating markets of the Mississippi and the bayous, selling china, making daguerreotypes, putting on shows, and providing first-class transportation for wealthy planters, complete with sumptuous meals and glamorous halls.

90/91 Cotton may no longer be king, but its cultivation and production remain a cornerstone of the economy in the Deep South.

92 Veterans don their tractor hats and American flags for a patriotic celebration of Independence Day, Southern style.

93 Ruby Malone tends her kitchen garden in Oxford, Mississippi, the haunt of William Faulkner, and the model for the mythical Yoknapatawpha County of his novels.

94/95 The Civil Rights Memorial in Montgomery delivers an eloquent eulogy for those who have given their lives for the cause of racial equality in the United States.

4·APR·1968   DR. MARTIN LUTHER KING
                ASSASSINATED·MEMPHIS

8·FEB·1968   SAMUEL HAMMOND JR·DEL
                MIDDLETON·HENRY SMITH·
                KILLED WHEN HIGHWAY PATR
                FIRED ON PROTESTERS·ORANG

2·OCT·1967   THURGOOD MARSHALL SWORN
                BLACK SUPREME COURT JUSTIC

                BENJAMIN BROWN·CIVIL RIGHT
12·MAY·1967   KILLED WHEN POLICE FIRED ON
                JACKSON, MS

                WHARLEST JACKSON·CIVIL RIG
                KILLED AFTER PROMOTION TO
27·FEB·1967   NATCHEZ, MS

                NCE TRIGGS·SLAIN B

...UNTIL JUSTICE ROLLS DOWN LIKE WATERS
AND RIGHTEOUSNESS LIKE A MIGHTY STREAM
MARTIN LUTHER KING JR.
STOP

96 Strong religious conviction is still very much a part of Southern life. Here, believers reaffirm their faith in a river baptism ceremony.

97 This Baptist church on Dexter Avenue in Montgomery was the birthplace of the civil rights movement in the United States. As its minister, Martin Luther King, Jr. preached some of the most stirring sermons ever delivered from its pulpit.

98 The graceful, cantilevered spiral staircases of the capitol building in Montgomery rise three stories without support. It was in this building that Jefferson Davis took his oath of office as president of the Confederacy.

99 The Confederate White House on Washington Avenue in Montgomery served as Jefferson Davis's headquarters during the formation of the Confederacy in 1861.

100/101 Huntsville became the hub of space and rocket research in the U.S. after World War II. The Space and Rocket Center is the world's largest space museum. The massive engines displayed here are from the Apollo Saturn V moon rocket.

102 Built by an industrialist, Bellingrath Home and Gardens in Alabama includes 800 acres of flowers, sculpture, and wildlife.

103 The feet of Indians, then of white settlers, wore the path of the Natchez Trace between Nashville, Tennessee and Natchez, Mississippi in the constant push westward during the 1800s. Now a scenic highway follows the Trace for much of its length.

104/105 The University of Alabama's Crimson Tide scores a field goal. Football competition is fierce in Alabama, with Auburn vying with U of A for the fans' affections.

LOUISIANA: CAJUN COUNTRY

Like a good bowl of gumbo, Louisiana mixes the flavors of its cultures into a unique whole. First explored by Hernando DeSoto in the early 1500s, Louisiana was passed back and forth between the Spanish and the French as a result of various wars and treaties until the United States acquired the territory in the Louisiana Purchase of 1803. Their legacy is seen today in the vibrant Creole culture they fostered, and in the division of the state into parishes instead of counties, a relic from the Catholic Church.

At the same time that France was establishing its Louisiana colony, English traders were moving west over Indian trails and down the Ohio River into the northern part of the territory. Settlers from the other southern colonies soon discovered the fertile alluvial soils of the Mississippi delta, and abandoned their worn-out farms in the Carolinas and Georgia.

Another group of settlers, the Acadians, were unwilling participants in the Louisiana experiment. Originally settled along the eastern coast of Canada, the French Acadians, or Cajuns, were forced on a treacherous exodus to the south when the British claimed Canada. Families were separated, and many died before the remaining Cajuns took up residence along the lazy waters of the bayous in the late 1700s. Today, the Cajun culture is a colorful mixture of the original French infused with Spanish, English, German, African, and Indian variations.

The Mississippi has always been a central part of Louisiana life. In addition to the Cajuns, the cheniers, or islands, of the Mississippi backwaters were the stomping grounds of Jean Lafitte and his pirate friends, who raided homes in the bayou as late as 1819 and created local rumors of buried treasure that still abound. The pirates were followed by deserters from the Confederate forces, who sought refuge from reinduction in the convolutions of Old Man River. Outside the shelter of the bayous, however, the Civil War wreaked havoc on the state. Quick to secede from the Union, Louisiana was equally quickly brought under Union control after the taking of New Orleans in 1862.

The discovery of oil in 1901 brought Louisiana's economy back to life, and since then, the state has flourished as one of the nation's biggest producers of petroleum and natural gas. In addition, it possesses 41 percent of the marshlands in the United States, an important breeding ground for the shellfish on which many people depend for their livelihood. The marshes and bayous also play host to thousands of migratory birds that travel the Mississippi flyway each winter, as well as to the human visitors who come to watch them.

New Orleans is the crown jewel of Louisiana. The heat of the climate is matched by the spice of New Orleans celebrations, the most famous being the excess of the annual Mardi Gras festival that precedes the austerity of Lent. The intricate ironwork of the houses, the sophistication of its hybrid society, and the jazz along Bourbon Street are just a sampling of what New Orleans has to offer.

A semi-tropical climate fills Louisiana with a multitude of flowering plants. Spanish moss drapes the live oak trees that border lanes leading to antebellum mansions. Beyond New Orleans, the countryside serves up its own spice, with zydeco music, French patois, jambalaya, and gumbo. Louisiana stands alone as the South's foreign-born cousin, giving residents and visitors alike a good dose of "bontemps," or good-time fun.

107 The graceful wings of a shrimp boat turn homeward at sunset. The shrimp fishing industry is an important source of employment for coast dwellers, including many Vietnamese immigrants who have made Louisiana home in recent years.

108/109 The annual blessing of the shrimp fleet begins a season of hard work for the fishermen of the Gulf.

110/111 A hallmark of the Deep South, Spanish moss graces the limbs of a live oak in Grand Coteau. The moss is a member of the pineapple family, native to the Americas.

112/113 A restored Acadian, or Cajun, village in Lafayette gives a feel for how the earliest settlers from French Canada started life on the bayou. Spanish, German, English, African, and Indian immigrants later joined these Frenchmen to form the unique Cajun culture of the Louisiana bayous.

114 Classic New Orleans architecture is the backdrop for the amicable mayhem of the annual Mardi Gras celebration.

115 The colorful whirl of a Mardi Gras float in New Orleans catches the attention of onlookers, who try to catch a prize of plastic bead necklaces as they are flung into the crowd.

116 The St. Charles Avenue streetcar conjures up images of Tennessee Williams's famed New Orleans denizens—Stanley Kowalski, Stella, and Blanche. This streetcar line is the oldest continually-operating line in the United States.

117 top Intricate ironwork is a trademark of New Orleans homes.

117 bottom Impromptu street jazz in New Orleans contributes to the city's reputation as a musical melting pot.

HUEY PIERCE LONG
1893 — 1935
GOVERNOR — 1928 — 1932
UNITED STATES SENATOR
1932 — 1935

HERE LIES LOUISIANA'S GREAT SON
HUEY PIERCE LONG AN UNCONQUERED
FRIEND OF THE POOR WHO DREAMED OF
THE DAY WHEN THE WEALTH OF THE LAND
WOULD BE SPREAD AMONG ALL THE PEOPLE

118 Huey P. Long's statue stands guard over the capitol grounds in Baton Rouge. The strongman of Louisiana politics from 1928-35, Long rose to power as a Populist. His proudest achievements were improvements in Louisiana's transportation, health care, and education systems.

119 Quarterback Jim McMahon signals a touchdown at Superbowl XX as the Chicago Bears steamroll the New England Patriots, 46-10 at Louisiana's Superdome.

120/121 First discovered in Louisiana in 1901, oil is an economic boon to the state. Louisiana is one of the nation's leading producers of oil and natural gas.

122/123 A zydeco music festival celebrates the unique cultural mix for which Louisiana is famous. Black Cajuns in the bayou further adapted the Cajun sound, putting their mark on the accordion-dominated melodies.